12.95    10/99

D0554629

# First Lady of the Air
## The Harriet Quimby Story

by

## Sterling Brown

Tudor Publishers
Greensboro

First Lady of the Air: The Harriet Quimby Story

Copyright © 1997 by Sterling Brown

Printed in the United States

First Edition

Library of Congress Cataloging-in-Publication Data

Brown, Sterling, 1948-
    First Lady of the Air: The Harriet Quimby Story/by Sterling Brown.—1st ed.
      p.      cm.
    Includes bibliograpical references and index.
    Summary: A biography of the pioneer aviatrix who was the first American woman to earn a pilot's license and to fly across the English Channel.
      ISBN 0-936389-49-4
      1. Quimby, Harriet, 1875-1912—Juvenile literature. 2. Women air pilots—United States—Biography—Juvenile literature. [1. Quimby, Harriet, 1875-1912. 2. Air pilots. 3. Women—Biography.]  I. Title
        TL540.Q496876                                          97-23405
        629.13'092—dc21                                            CIP
        [B]                                                          AC

To my wife, Dawn

# Contents

# Chapter 1

## A Michigan Farm Girl

Harriet reached into her sack, grabbed a handful of cornmeal and threw it at the chickens. The dry grain pelted their backs, but they didn't seem to mind. They pecked at the ground around Harriet's feet, and stretched their useless wings. She laughed. "Mom," she shouted toward the farm house, "look at these old birds."

Harriet's mother stood on the porch. Old birds, Ursula Quimby thought. Chickens weren't any kind of bird at all. They were only good for eggs and dinner. A bird was a creature that lived in the air.

"If they had good sense," she shouted back at Harriet, "they'd fly off."

And so would we, Ursula thought. She leaned on the porch rail and shook her head. Fly or walk, she and her family might soon be leaving. The mortgage on the farm was overdue, and the bank was threatening to foreclose. Unless the Quimbys extended their loan, in a few weeks the bank would own everything, porch, house and land. Well, Ursula thought, let it be. Let the bank take the farm, and it could take these Michigan winters, too. The Quimbys had been working their land for years, and what did they have to show for it? Two daughters and some chickens.

Ursula smiled. Now the daughters, they were worth it, all the hardship and frustration. There was Harriet in her blue gingham dress. Harriet, dark-eyed and at nine and nearly as tall as her fourteen-year-old sister Kitty. Harriet, laughing as the chickens pecked at her toes.

Ursula looked past the child to the edge of the yard where the trees reached up toward the sky. Somewhere beneath it, Ursula was sure, was a place where she and her family could find a better life, where the Quimbys would not have to scratch the ground. The barn door slammed, and Ursula saw her husband William walking toward her. He looked so tired, she thought. Tonight they would talk about leaving.

Satisfied with her decision, Ursula stepped back from the rail and turned to go inside. As she did, Harriet threw the last of the cornmeal into the air. It fell around her and she laughed and ran toward her mother, her arms outstretched. Ursula stretched hers out also.

"Mama," Harriet called to her. "Look at me. I can fly!"

A few weeks later, in the spring of 1884, the Quimbys were on a train heading west. Harriet and Kitty looked wide-eyed out the windows at the land passing by: towering forests, fields of wheat and corn, prairies that seemed to stretch forever. The train climbed slowly through rugged mountains, chugged along the edges of sheer cliffs, and the girls stared out at the silver ribbons of rivers twisting in the valleys far below. "We're too high!" Kitty gasped, but Harriet did not seem to hear her. She had never looked down on things before. Even the farmhouse had been only one story. She saw the world now in a new way. It was much bigger and more grand than she had ever realized. No one had told her this, that the world wasn't comprised merely of barns and porched houses...and chicken yards. There was so much to see! And what a lovely way to see it, from the air. As the train entered into the lush valleys of California, Harriet placed her hand above her heart and made a promise to herself. She would find her way into the sky again, and see the world once more as she had just seen it

After arriving by stagecoarch in a town called
Arroyo Grande, the Quimbys again tried farming,
then spent the last of their small savings opening
a general store. California, the family agreed, was
a fine state. A few years later, California was still
a fine state, but the state of the Quimby's financ-
es had become desperate. They were broke. Ursula
again stood on a porch, this time her store's. She
thought again about her daughters. Kitty had married in 1887, and was now on her own. But Harriet
was still young and needed Ursula's guidance. She
shouldn't come to maturity knowing only failure.
If Arroyo Grande was not where the Quimbys could
succeed, then perhaps another town would be. A
larger town, a place with more opportunities.
Suddenly, Ursula knew the answer.

"William," she called out to her husband, "we
need to talk again."

There had been nothing in Michigan like San
Francisco. It was big and bright and clean, built on
hills by the bay. The Quimbys were now partners
with Ursula's brother in the patent medicine business. The medicine, according to the label, would
cure everything from arthritis to ringworm. While

Harriet helped Ursula bottle the elixir, William traversed the city selling it from the back of a wagon. For the first time in their lives, things started looking up. Ursula was soon able to stand on the stoop of their apartment building and say, "This is good." Then she would go inside and fix a chicken dinner.

It was at mealtime that Ursula's determination seemed strongest. "Now listen," she would say to her daughter. "Life is a risk. The person who takes a chance is a person who has a chance."

"Yes, Mama," Harriet would say.

" A woman is the equal of any man," Ursula continued, looking over at at William, who silently read the *San Francisco Chronicle*. "But she has to work harder than any man if she wants to make her mark."

"Yes, Mama,"

"And a woman can make her mark, I promise, if she takes advantage of life, and works as hard as she can, and has daring..."

There was a pause.

"And what, Mama?"

"And never forgets," Ursula said, raising a ladle damp with gravy, "never, that she's a lady."

Young Harriet nodded her head solemnly. "Mama," she said. "I won't forget."

# Chapter 2

## "I'll Be A Writer"

Years passed quickly. Harriet was in her twenties now, older than Kitty had been when she married. Ursula looked at her daughter and realized that soon she might wish to marry, too. That was as it should be, Ursula thought. But if Harriet was to marry, at least let her marry well, very well.

This posed a problem. The obscure daughters of failed farmers had few advantages when seeking the type of husband Ursula had in mind. There was only one solution: Harriet's parents had not failed. Why, of course not. Harriet, as Ursula began telling everyone, had been born in Boston and educated in Europe, and the Quimbys were a wealthy farming family from northern  California.

"But Mother..." Harriet protested.

" 'But, Mother' nothing," Ursula said. "You'll be accepted into society. There are things which society wants to hear, and it *will* hear them. From now on, Michigan to you is only a name on a map."

Harriet, now taller than her mother, looked down into her eyes. Her white teeth showed as she smiled. "That's right," she said softly. "Only a name."

Although Harriet was a good and hard-working daughter, she soon realized that a marriage and children were not what she wanted. Yes, she wanted a good life. But she wanted her life to be free. A husband and children would hold her back, tie her down. That was not for her; she wanted something more. It came as little surprise, then, when Harriet decided in 1900 to become something few women before her had been.

"I'll be a writer," she announced when she was twenty-six.

Harriet soon won a job as a theatre critic on the *San Francisco Drama Review.* With the diligence she had shown in the family patent medicine business, she began writing articles about plays and concert sthroughout the city. Backstage, she interviewed the musicians and actors. She even talked to the ushers. In this way, she gained a great appreciation for the efforts behind the entertainments she covered. At the same time she also began writing feature stories for the *Call-Bulletin* and the *Chronicle.* These stories made her quite popular in San Francisco. Readers enjoyed the freshness and enthusiasm which Harriet brought to her writing.

It seemed that she was willing to try anything, even in the writing itself; reportedly, she was one of the first of her profession to use a typewriter.

Harriet had another thing in her favor. Certainly, she was unique and intelligent, but she was also beautiful. The photographs that remain show a slender, high-cheekboned woman with wide-set eyes, a charming smile. Some people say she was much sought after as an artist's model, and it is known that her portrait hung in San Francisco's all-male Bohemian Club, adored by the members, until the 1906 earthquake destroyed the building.

Despite her popularity, Harriet eventually decided to move to New York City. The West had brought success, but the East might bring more. She wanted more money, because her goal was to retire at thirty-five and write "a novel or two." Ursula agreed, and concluded that her daughter would be better off arriving in New York at the age of eighteen. Twenty-seven was old. Her logic was simple; the younger Harriet was, the more opportunities she would find. So, by the time Harriet Quimby arrived alone in New York City, the year of her birth had been changed from 1875 to 1884.

In 1902, women worked hard, but few were employed. They usually labored at home, without pay. Of those who had salaried jobs, not many were writers. Writing was supposed to be "man's work," and Harriet was initially able to find work in New York only as a freelancer. That meant she did not have a steady, guaranteed job. Her income fluctuated. One month she might make ten dollars, the next month, $200. It depended on how many articles she sold.

*Leslie's Weekly* bought most of them. *Leslie's* was a widely-read national news magazine, selling 325,000 copies per week for ten cents. Harriet wrote all sorts of articles for *Leslie's*. Her fascination with the different ways that people lived is evident in one of her stories, "Curious Chinese Customs." She also wrote about women's issues and the freedoms they were starting to secure. Fashion, travel and the environment were other favored topics. One article warned of the extinction of homing pigeons and song birds.

In 1906, *Leslie's* sent their leading female journalist, Eleanor Franklin, on a writing tour. Harriet filled in for her, and had done so well by the end of the year that the magazine hired her as a full-time reporter. This was what she had been waiting for. Now she would have enough money to bring her parents to live with her. Soon, Ursula, now seventy-two, moved in with Harriet at the Hotel Victoria on Broadway in Manhattan. William, however, decided to remain in California.

By the end of 1906, Harriet had written more than 100 articles for *Leslie's*, frequently illustrating them with photographs she took. Her position as a journalist was secure and she was quickly becoming one of the best-known female writers of her time. Three years passed. Then, in 1909, she wrote an article which would have great significance in her life. It was called, "A Japanese Aeronaut To Startle The World." From that time on, Harriet was never the same. Neither, it could be argued, was aviation.

# Chapter 3

## The Black-Veiled Student

By age thirty-five, Harriet had become a regular visitor at airfields, or "getaways." In 1910 she went to Belmont Park race track to cover an international air meet. Many famous flyers were competing in a series of events culminating in the Statue of Liberty Race, a thirty-six-mile time trial across the harbor to the statue and back. John Bevins Moisant was the foremost American competitor. The crowd wanted this dapper, handsome "swashbuckler of the air" to win. but they didn't think he could; his plane was too slow, and he had already crashed once. Moisant, however, was determined to beat the odds-on favorite, an Englishman named Claude Grahame-White.

He did so, but not without a few problems. during the race, Moisant crashed into another plane, wrecking his single-wing Bleriot. Unhurt, he bought a new plane and, after the race was over and the victor declared, took off again.

17

There were no crashes this time, but Moisant flew so boldly that some said his wing clipped the statue as he went around it. When he landed, he had shaved forty-three seconds off the course record. In a startling reversal, the judges declared him the winner.

The original winner wasn't happy about the judges' decision, particularly since Moisant now was awarded the $10,000 prize. And who was that winner? Claude Grahame-White.

The crowd was thrilled with Moisant. They draped an American flag around his shoulders and carried him across the field. Harriet, watching all this, could not wait to interview him.

John Moisant became her hero. She decided she wanted to be like him. The immediate problem, of course, was that she could not fly an airplane. But, remembering Ursula's advice, she was certain she could learn.

Moisant, however, was not interested in teaching her. Like most men, he thought that women belonged on the ground. But Harriet ignored that attitude. She was determined to get into the air, and refused to relent in her goal. Finally, Moisant agreed to teach her soon, after opening his flying school. But, unfortunately, that never came to be. On December 31, 1911, from a height of 100 feet, John

Moisant fell from his plane during an exhibition in New Orleans. His death upset Harriet greatly. However, it did not stop her from signing up for lessons at the Moisant Aviation School in Hempstead Plains, New York, on May 10, her birthday. Moisant's brother Alfred ran the school, which had opened a few months earlier. His sister Matilde also took lessons. She and Harriet became friends.

On the evenings before her lessons, Harriet, as one of the first licensed female drivers in New York City, would drive her little red roadster out to the Garden City Hotel near the airfield. There she would take a room. The Garden City was one of the few hotels to have a telephone in each room. If the wind was under five miles per hour, and if it wasn't raining or too cold, and if an airplane and a teacher were available, the telephone would wake Harriet at four o'clock a.m.

After a quick breakfast, she would drive to the flying school in her little red roadster. By 5:30, just as dawn was breaking, she would step onto the airfield, ready to begin. At first her instructors must not have known what to make of her. The writer's usual attire on these early mornings was a man's knickerbocker suit (a one-piece coverall that buttoned up the front like a mechanic's overalls), a leather skull cap (like a bathing cap with a strap under the chin), goggles, gloves and high-laced boots. She also wore an item that set her apart. Around her head, and fastened at her neck, was a black veil. Harriet could see out, but her face was obscured. Although the airfield personnel knew the identity of the new student, the other pilots-in-training must have stared at her, trying to decide who she might be. And that, of course, was what Harriet wanted. She liked calling attention to herself, but was unsure about letting her readers know she was taking flying lessons.

The mystery ended on May 10th when a newspaper reporter visiting the airfield realized who she was and revealed it in a story. Did Harriet help him in his realization? We can only guess.

Apart from the veil, Harriet's aviation clothing made sense. In 1911, most women wore long skirts. But skirts were not good for flying. Airplane cockpits were roofless, and a skirt could blow up in a pilot's face and wrap around the wires supporting the wings. A woman could tie the hem around her ankles, as some later did, but that restricted foot movement, preventing her from pushing the rudder pedals.Wide hats also were a problem; they were like wearng a parachute. Then there was the oil. The loud and loose three-cylnder engines were lubricated with caster oil, which, spraying from leaky gaskets and the exhaust manifold, eventually also lubricated the pilot, covering his clothes and face. Considering all this, Harriet was sensibly dressed.

It wasn't long, though, before Harriet had created her own special flying costume. With Alex Graen, president of the New York Tailor's Association, she designed what would be called the first "jump-suit." It was  like a knickerbocker, but better. The one-piece suit was made of mauve satin and lined with soft wool. It buttoned under the arms, was drawn in at the waist, and the skirt gathered into leggings which fit into her boots. A monk-like hood attached at the neck. Two small circles of mesh by her ears permitted Harriet to hear engine sounds. She looked exquisite in this suit, very "dashing," as people said, with her gauntlet gloves and almond-shaped goggles. In winter she wore a sleek leather coat over her outfit, and in the summer a mauve cape. Her attire, along with Harriet, became quite famous.

# Chapter 4

## Grass-Cutting And Kangarooing

On a soft May morning in 1911, Harriet's jump-suit was months away. Her clothing at this point was of small concern. She was here to fly. *Leslie's Weekly* had paid $750 for her lessons, which she would earn by the articles she had agreed to write. Her editors knew what they were doing. The public had a growing fascination with this fad called flying, and avidly read anything written about it. Now, with a first-person account of a woman's ascension into the air, *Leslie's* circulation was sure to ascend as well.

But now it was the sun that was rising, giving the air a pink glow. Harriet knelt to pet the school's mascot, a little white dog with a black spot on his forehead. "Sleepy, boy?" she asked. "I know, I know." The little dog yawned.

Other students arrived, and each went to the hangar and carried a chair onto the field. Ground school was about to begin. The instructor, a tall man meticulously dressed in a dark suit and tie, followed them out. His name was Andre Houpert, whom his students fondly referred to as "the Professor." The title fit him as well as his round bowler hat.

Houpert took his work very seriously. This business of flying was brand new. It was exhileration; it was wonderful, and it was extremely dangerous. Many would die, Houpert knew. Conceivably one of these students, perhaps the lovely young woman with the dark hair, mght be among them. If there was a way to avoid that, the professor meant to find that way. In his measured Gallic accent, Houpert, as on the day before, carefully went over the first week's topics: The theories of flight and of basic airplane construction.

This instruction was far differrent from what pilots learn today. Many early planes had only a control stick and rudder pedals. There were no brake pedals, because there were no brakes. Except on the most advanced airplanes, there were no airlerons— adjustable wing flaps for balance and lateral control. Instrumentation was rudimentary; sometimes an altimeter and a wind-speed indicator, at other times nothing at all. This lack of technology meant that aviation then was what we might consider primitive, but ground school was no less important than now. In some ways it was more so. Planes were much less dependable than they are today, much less safe, and time spent on the ground prepared a pilot, hopefully, for emergencies he would meet when above it.

The training went well, as it did each morning thereafter. During the second week a plane was taken apart and reassembled. During week three the students climbed into a flight simulator, a machine, bolted to the hanger floor that rotated and tilted similar an airplane.

An important part of the training was learning how to use the ignition switch. The chief mechanic took a special interest in this lesson. When a plane was started, his job was to spin the propeller. If the pilot turned on the ignition too soon, the mechanic could be injured by the rotating propeller blade.

"Grass-cutting" was saved for the fourth week. This was simply the taxiing of a short-winged airplane from one end of the airfield to the other. The plane, with two wheels in the front and a skid in the rear, was unable to rise more than two or three feet from the ground.

Before each lesson, the professor would test the wind. His method was simple. He would blow cigar smoke, wave a handkerchief, or watch the flapping of a flag atop a nearby pole. If he needed more accuracy, he examined a hand-held instrument called an anemometer. It looked like a windmill with cups instead of paddles. If the cups spun too fast, he would say, slowly, "We must wait."

After learning to "grass-cut," Harriet graduated to "kangarooing" in a longer-winged plane, which could make little hops, four or five feet high. Soon she was an accomplished kangarooer.

"Now I'm ready to hop into the air," she said to the professor, "and stay there."

The professor looked at her closely. "Everyone," he said, "must come down."

Harriet's first big hop came the next week. This was the week of the "supervised solo." Her plane, a 30-horsepower single-wing Moisant, had a device fitted to the tail that limited its altitude. Harriet learned to "climb" in this plane, bank to the right or left and, of course, fly in a straight line. She practiced "figure-eights."

She and all the students had to learn to "cut a pathway" through the air. This was accomplished by twisting the control stick, which, with the use of warped cables, literally warped the wings into shape to navigate the plane. Such navigation was as difficult as it sounds, and crashes were not infrequent. The biggest chance of crashing came when the student tried to land. Imagine trying to land a wobbling, wooden, canvas-clad, screaming-loud airplane that is spitting oil in your face. If you can do that, you'll have some idea of Harriet's first solo.

# Chapter 5

## The Test

After thirty-three lessons over two months, the young writer was ready take the test for her license. In the early morning of July 31, two judges from the Aeronautic Club of America were waiting. Harriet climbed into the cockpit. Four mechanics held the tail wing. The head mechanic spun the propeller. Harriet turned the ignition switch and the engine roared to life. When the propeller had reached sufficient revolutions to pull the plane, the mechanics let go. The plane slid forward, gaining speed, and Harriet pulled back on the control stick and the plane lifted into the air. Suddenly, it seemed she was high above them, high above the judges, the other students, her instructors, and high above the field, the hangar, the flag on the pole. She looked past the wing, out across the land, out through the cool morning air, and she knew she was where she wanted to be. She was flying.

All went well in the first part of the test. Harriet

appeared confident. The plane flew steadily, banking through five figure-eights. Then it dropped in altitude and Harriet prepared to come in for a landing. But, having done everything correctly, she forgot to cut her engine at the right moment, Each student was required to land within 165 feet of a mark on the field. Harriet missed the mark by 205 feet. She stood by the plane wiping oil from her face, but she was also wiping tears.

"Please," she said to the judges, "let me try again." They might have allowed her to, but the wind had now picked up. She would get a second chance the next day.

It seemed that the morrow would never arrive. Finally, however, the sun rose higher, then fell, and night came and passed, and in Harriet's hotel room the telephone rang. It was 4:30 on the morning of August 1, 1911.

Professor Houpert said, "The fog is thick enough to cut with a knife. Don't come over until I send my motor car for you when the field is clear."

Harriet dressed and had breakfast with her friend Matilde Moisant in the hotel's lobby. The judges arrived. They had arranged the night before for a car to take everyone to the airfield. Without waiting for the Professor to call , they and Harriet and Matilde got into the car. When they showed up at the airfield he was obviously annoyed. "We must wait," he said stiffly. It was still foggy, with no signs of clearing. Everyone paced. The chief mechanic was encouraging. "When the sun rises," he said, "the fog will disappear." He was right; by 6:00 a. m. conditions had improved enough that a plane was wheeled from the hangar.

Harriet and Matilde had decided to take the test the same day. Matilde, aware of her companion's ambitions, insisted Harriet go on. Harriet wanted Matilde to go first. "I can't wait," she said. This time, five mechanics held the tail. The engine sputtered, and roared, spewing oil-filled smoke. Harriet's face was hidden in the thick white cloud. Moments passed while the propeller spun faster and faster. Finally, Harriet gave the thumbs-up sign. The mechanics released her, she waved goodbye, the plane made a few hops across the field, and she was up. Quickly she reached an altitude of 150 feet.

Again, Harriet made five figure-eights. Poles at either end of the field designated where she was to bank to the right or left. A judge stood at each pole. Professor Houpert placed himself where she could see him. He had said he would wave his handkerchief when she finished her last turn. Harriet, high above, was confident of her flying skills but less confident of her engine. She hoped it would run strongly and not force her to land. She had never "pancaked" a plane before, and didn't want to have to today. But the little engine ran well, Harriet completed the eights, Professor Houpert waved proudly, and she landed without a problem.

While the overheated engine cooled, everyone congratulated her. Soon she and the engine were ready to fly again. A white circular cloth was spread out on the field. Before she took off, Harriet stood looking at it. She would be retested on her landing skill, and she did not want a repeat of the day before. Without brakes, Harriet would have to be very careful if she was to land within 165 feet of the cloth. The judges watched her fly away again, watched her circle the field, and watched her cautiously land. Harriet was smiling as she stepped from the plane. The judges smiled too. After measuring the distance, the plane was only seven feet, nine inches from the cloth! Harriet had just set a record for landing in a monoplane. The judges were amazed. If Harriet was, she kept it to herself.

For her final requirement, Harriet would have to fly to an altitude of 164 feet. An altimeter in the plane would record her attempt. Still smiling, she took off. Harriet was certain now that she would win her license. After ascending in a series of spirals, she dropped easily to earth. Eagerly, the judges approached the plane. Now was their chance to be amazed again. Harriet had reached an altitude of 220 feet. She had never gone this high before; she was used to flying at the test height of 164.

"I guess I get that license," she said, beaming at the judges.

"You certainly do," they replied. Harriet, one of the best-known journalists in the United States, was about to become its first licensed female pilot.

She would also be the first person in the world to earn a license in a monoplane. It was a remarkable achievement. In all, during her brief training flights. Harriet had spent less than two hours in the air.

A number of news reporters were present to record the event. One asked how she felt now about flying.

"It's not a fad," she replied. "And I didn't want to be the first American woman to fly just to make myself conspicuous. I just wanted to be first, that's all, and I honestly and frankly am delighted. I have written so much about other people, you can't guess how much I enjoy sitting back and reading about myself for once. I think that's excusable in me."

Having said that, Harriet rushed off to change from her brown shirt and trousers, skull cap and goggles into clean clothes. She was covered with castor oil.

When she returned, Matilde was about to take the test. Her plane sat next to Harriet's. Nearby was a large group of oil cans. As the judges waited, Matilde headed toward her airplane. Suddenly she realized that another plane was heading toward her. A pilot named W. G. Beattie had decided to observe the proceedings. W. G. should have stayed home. He had come to see Harriet get her license, but he didn't have his own yet.

"Look out!" someone yelled to Matilde. It was too late. She stared open-mouthed as W. G. attempted to taxi between her plane and the oil cans. Unfortunately, he missed the cans. With a sickening, splintering crash, W. G.'s plane rammed into Matilde's, wrecking its tail rudder.

He also wrecked Matilde's chance of taking the test that day. She would have to wait. At least she was not hurt. And W. G.? He was fine.

"Come on," Harriet said to cheer her up. "I'll buy you breakfast."

"We've already had breakfast," replied a very dejected Matilde

"Then you buy me lunch," responded Harriet.

# Chapter 6

## For The Love Of Flying

Matilde waited over a week while the plane was repaired. High winds prevented the test on August 12th. Then, the next day, she flew five figure-eights at an altitude of seventy-five feet, landing seventy-one feet, four inches, from the mark. Her license was number 44, making her the second American female pilot.

"We won't take chances," she said afterward to a reporter. "We'll show them we can fly, and we won't break either the machines or our necks in doing it."

Harriet was equally determined to prove her flying skill. To do so, she decided, she would need her own plane. A good one would cost between five and six thousand dollars, quite a lot of money in 1911. She knew she could use her new license to earn the money. As a journalist, she also knew she could use it to earn fame, which would bring the money faster. About a month after passing her test,

Harriet became the first person to fly at night, at the Richmond County Fair in Dongan Hills, Staten Island. Twenty thousand people filled the airfield to watch her. Before she could take off, she had to clear spectators from the landing strip with her car. She then flew out over the Narrows and back to Staten Island. This was followed by a series of circles above the crowd. Then Harriet swooped down over the grandstand. Hearing the crowd's applause, she circled again. From her wicker seat she waved a white handkerchief.

Now it was time to land, and she began her descent. But as Harriet neared the ground, she realized she was in trouble. The crowd, wildly enthused, had again run onto the field. There seemed to be nowhere to land. At the last moment she flew over their heads and dropped down behind them, almost crashing into a fence. She nearly was thrown from her seat. Luckily, the plane broke only a few wires.

Ursula rushed across the field, grabbed her daughter and held her. "You were up just seven minutes, Harriet, and I think I would have come up after you if you had remained any longer."

"Oh, Mother," Harriet said, "you'll get used to it. It was grand. I didn't feel like ever coming to earth again."

During her early flights, the press criticized Harriet for only making short "hops." This stopped, though, when the distances lengthened to twenty miles or more. In September of 1911, she flew a prolonged demonstration flight at the Trenton State Fair for a fee of $1,500, setting the American endurance record for women. At the Nassau Boulevard Tournament in New York, Harriet was prepared to defend her record against aviatrix Hélène Dutrieu. But the meet was scheduled on a Sunday.

"I promised my mother I would not fly on the Sabbath," she told the organizers.

She kept her promise. Madam Hélène Dutrieu broke Harriet's record by many minutes. Harriet, who had watched from a nearby hangar, said afterward that she was unconcerned about losing the record. "A record won on a Sunday would not be worthwhile," she said.

Later she won a cross-country race against her rival, Mdm. Dutrieu, and received $600. She also received an offer to fly in a Chicago air meet, but turned it down when officials were unable to pay what she asked. Two fatal crashes occurred at this event. A flyer who attended later told her, "You should consider yourself lucky the Chicago committee didn't come up to your price. The tournament grounds were the worst I've ever seen."

Had she been lucky? she wondered. Was the risk of flying, no matter how much she loved it, worth the money? This was a sport in which people died. John Moisant was one of the best flyers she had ever seen. One moment he had been soaring above the crowd, aloft in the sky. The next moment he had crashed to earth. John had been a wonderful man. Harriet had wanted to be just like him. Did she want to be dead, too? Was any amount of money worth the risk of ending up like John?

As she thought about this, Harriet realized it really was not the money she desired. And it wasn't the fame, either. Money and fame could do nothing for John now. Nor would it help the two men who had died in Chicago. No, as had those men, she knew now that she truly loved to fly. All her life, it seemed, she had been glued to the earth. She had been held to it, pressed down upon it. And now she was able to lift from it high into the air. And if she fell, that was a risk worth taking. Fear would never stop her. But when she flew for hire, people would pay what it was worth. She would fly for the love of flying, and die if she had to, but she would not fly for less than she deserved.

\*　　\*　　\*　　\*　　\*

Toward the end of October, 1911, Harriet and

Matilde, with the rest of the Moisant International Aviators, went to Mexico on the liner *Lampasa*. They took the mechanics, six monoplanes, and two biplanes. In 1910, John and his brother Alfred had founded the team to promote the Moisant aeroplane by giving exhibitions. The Moisants also helped to generate interest in flying schools they hoped to create throughout the United States.

The team had been asked to fly during the inaugural ceremonies of Mexico's President Maderos. They were to receive $100,000 for the performance. Harriet again achieved another first, the first woman to fly over Mexico. She also was almost the first woman to fly *into* Mexico; on one of her flights her engine failed at 150 feet, forcing her to make an emergency landing.

It may have been in Mexico that Harriet found one of her favorite lucky charms. She loved jewelry, and often decided that one piece or other would bring her good fortune. Her new Mexican necklace, which she began wearing when she flew, consisted of a small clay head, the supposed likeness of an Aztec king, suspended by a silver chain. She enjoyed telling people that it was 2000 years old.

The Moisant team had planned to spend the winter south of the border, but their trip was cut short when Mexico's revolution began. Not all of the heat in Mexico, they realized, was coming from the sun. Quickly, the flyers headed back to cold New York.

# Chapter 7

## Fly The Channel

Harriet returned to the usual debate about flying and danger, specifically about women, flying and danger. In response, perhaps forcing the issue somewhat, she wrote:

"Flying is easier than walking, automobiling, golf, or tennis. Over a good flying ground on a calm day, driving an aeroplane is as safe as driving an automobile in a crowded city. Over ground filled with holes and ruts which send up gusty whirlpools and cause treacherous "air-pockets," aeroplaning becomes hazardous. Yet with a clear-headed pilot, it need not be necessarily dangerous. Flying is a fine, dignified sport for women, healthful and stimulating to the mind and there is no reason to be afraid as long as she is careful."

"Careful" was an important word to Harriet, who constantly sought ways to make flying safe. She insisted on always inspecting her aircraft prior to flight, and advised all pilots to follow a pre-flight checklist. Ironically, as it turned out, she also advised them to wear seat belts. And she never stopped believing that no one should fly on Sunday. This advice only added to her reputation, and by January of 1912 she had become *Leslie's* aviation editor.

Her mother's mathematics notwithstanding, Harriet was now thirty-seven years old. For a woman of her era, she had had a most unusual life. She had traveled, written, and flown airplanes. It had been exciting, and the public had not failed to notice. Shy men sent her anonymous poetry. Others sent marriage proposals. Flowers, jewelry, and all sorts of other gifts descended upon her from admirers. She returned them when possible, with a note of appreciation. The acceptance of gifts from strangers, she believed, would cast a shadow on her character.

Harriet preferred to cast a shadow on the land. To do that, she had to fly. The average man would only get in the way. But then she met a different kind of man. "You need to set another 'first,' " he told her. "I can help you do it."

Harriet agreed. Leo Stevens became her manager.

Leo was a balloon pilot. He designed and produced them in a foundry he owned. He held the nation's second balloon pilot license. A friend of the aviation pioneering Wright brothers, he would eventually become one of the Army's first civilian aircraft inspectors.

Leo was a handsome man, dark-haired, with a friendly smile. He liked Harriet and did not want her to get hurt, but he understood her love of flying and her driving ambition.

"Look," he said to her at lunch one day, "this thing, it has to grab the public."

"Grab the public," Harriet repeated. "Yes, of course." They were in a small New York café, sipping tea.

"That's right," Leo said. "Like this," squeezing his chicken sandwich.

"Don't, you'll bruise it," said Harriet.

"You need to fly over something big," Leo continued. "This table, for instance." He "flew" the sandwich across the tablecloth.

"If only it were that easy," Harriet sighed.

"Well, that's what you need to do," Leo said. He landed the sandwich onto a blue china plate.

"What a wonderful way to fly," Harriet teased. "You'd never go hungry."

"If we get this right, hunger is the last thing you will have to worry about."

"Something big," mulled Harriet, looking at him

across the table.

"Nothing less," Leo said.

"That's easy," Harriet replied. "France is lovely in the spring."

And so they decided: Harriet would fly across
the English Channel.

The first person to do so was Louis Bleriot, on
July 25, 1909. Bleriot, born in 1872, had become
one of the foremost manufacturers of airplanes in
the world. On his Channel flight, he piloted his 23-
horsepower Bleriot XI, leaving Baraques, France,
at 4:41 a.m., and landing thirty-six-and-a-half minutes later in Northfall Meadow, near Dover Castle,
England.

John Moisant became the first American to fly
the Channel when he crossed later that year. His
route was from Dover to Calais, the opposite of
Bleriot. Harriet agreed with Moisant's logic. Thinking of Dover's white cliffs, she said, "It seems to
be the route I should take. The cliffs are higher."

Regardless of the direction Harriet might take,
the Channel was the same frightening width— more
than twenty miles. The first woman to fly over it
would, as Leo had said, "grab" the attention of both
the public and other aviators. She would become
a part of history. Of course, she might also become
part of the English Channel. Many pilots had al-

ready perished in attempted crossings. Simply flying a plane across an airfield was dangerous; flying across the Channel's open expanse was nothing short of foolhardy. But Harriet was willing to take the risk. She and Leo started their plans, which they kept secret. They did not want another woman to get the idea, too.

Harriet knew that Bleriot's help would be invaluable. Leo obtained a letter of introduction to the aeronaut, and he and Harriet departed for England. She wrote, "On the seventh of March I sailed on the Hamburg-American liner, *Amerika*, went to London and disclosed my project to the wide-awake editor of the *London Mirror*. He was delighted with the idea and immediately offered me a handsome inducement if I would make the trip as the *Mirror's* representative." Harriet was again in need of money. This venture would not be cheap. With a $5,000 advance from England's biggest newspaper, she and Leo set off to visit Louis Bleriot.

She also took with her a small charm she had seen in the news room of the *Mirror*. It was a brass figure on a necklace, a depiction of the east Indian god Ganesha. The *Mirror* had recently asked readers to send in lucky charms that no longer brought good luck. Ganesha was one of many that came through the mail, and Harriet found it in a pile on a desk. She had never seen anything quite like it before, with its elephant head on a man's fat body, crossed legs, and three arms holding a hook, a stone and an axe.

"What an odd little beast," she said to a copy boy who was passing.

"Yes, ma'am," he agreed. "A regular devil, I'd wager."

"You would, would you?" she asked, lifting the charm into the light. The eyes of the elephant head seemed to wink at her. "I don't think he's a devil at all," she said to the boy. "Just misunderstood."

The boy was unconvinced. "A devil, for my money," he insisted. Then a reporter called for him, and he ran off.

"Just misunderstood," Harriet repeated. Carrying the charm, she returned to the office of the editor. A minute later, Ganesha was hers.

A confident Harriet seated in the cockpit of her Moisant Bleriot XI, 1912. (*Courtesy: Smithsonian Institution. National Air and Space Museum*).

Matilde Moisant (center left) and Harriet listen with other students to Andre Houpert (*Courtesy: Smithsonian Institution. National Air and Space Museum*).

Harriet as a correspondent for *Leslie's Weekly Magazine. (Courtesy: National Air and Space Museum. Smithsonian Institution).*

Leo Hamel give Harriet last minute advice before her flight across the English Channel, April 16, 1912. (Courtesy: *Smithsonian Institution. National Air and Space Museum*).

# Chapter 8

## Today Is The Day

Louis Bleriot was a stout, hearty Frenchman with a drooping black moustache. He owned a grand home in Paris, and Harriet and Leo visited them there the first week of April. When Harriet said that she wanted to buy Bleriot's most powerful plane, a seventy-horse-power model, he raised his broad hands in frustration. "I want to help you," he said, "but I only have a fifty-horse-power aeroplane."

Leo refused to be discouraged. "What if we use it until a seventy is ready?"

Harriet smiled. "Yes," she said, looking across the parlor from Leo to the Frenchman. "Oh, Monsieur Bleriot, I think that's a wonderful idea."

Evidently Bleriot thought so too, because he immediately agreed to accept a $5,000 promissory note for the seventy-horsepower plane. If Harriet were to damage the fifty, the money would pay for it instead.

There was a good chance of this happening,

because Harriet had decided to use the fifty for the Channel crossing. "You should test the plane first," Bleriot advised, and Leo agreed.

Bleriot's summer residence was in Hardelot, France, a few miles from the Channel. Adjacent to his house, he owned an airstrip with a hangar. It seemed prudent to Harriet that the test take place there, where it would arouse the least suspicion. Without delay, she and Leo traveled to Hardelot After renting separate rooms in a small hotel, they waited.

Three days later they were still waiting; it had rained since their arrival. "Time was flying—even if I was not," Harriet wrote later. Finally it was too late. She had to ship the plane back to Dover. Her wire to the *Mirror* requested that photographers and reporters meet her at the Hotel Lord Warden, where she registered as a "Miss Craig." Leo and Harriet remained cautious, afraid someone would learn of their plans and try to beat them. They were right.

While she had tarried in France, a French pilot named Gustav Hamel had flown an Englishwoman, Eleanor Trehawk Davis, across the Channel. Miss Davis had hired Hamel to make this flight in her Bleriot. Even though Miss Davis was only a passenger, Harriet was very disappointed to learn that another woman had beaten her across the Channel.

Her disappoint-ment increased when the *Mirror* withdrew its finan-cial support.

Now, with so much having gone wrong, Harriet was not sure what to do. She remained that way only briefly, however. "I'll do it anyway," she told Leo.

"Of course you will," he said. "I have never thought you wouldn't."

The weather on Aril 14, 1912, was perfect: calm and clear. But Harriet had promised never to fly on a Sunday, and remained true to her word. Hamel, who had insinuated himself into the Quimby party, took the Bleriot up for what he called a "shakedown" flight. Onlookers gathered. Reporters came and left. Hamel said that he was the one preparing for the flight. Harriet tried to cover up rumors about her attempt to fly the Channel. She and Leo circulated several of their own to throw reporters off the trail. Gaumont Cinematograph Company of London took moving pictures of Gustav Hamel. Harriet, with Leo and their crew, returned to the hotel at 7:00 p. m. The *London Mirror's* staff aboard a news tug, and would-be flight witnesses in Calais, were disgruntled. Hamel seemed more so than anyone. "I'll make the flight for you," he offered. "Let me wear your purple suit." He explained that Harriet could wait in Calais and change places (and clothes) with him when he landed.

For the first time in days, Harriet laughed. "Only if you wear my perfume," she said, waving his idea away.

Harriet had great trust in herself, but little in Hamel. Later in *World Magazine*, she claimed she had told him about her plans two days before he had ferried Miss Davis across the Channel. He had robbed her, she said, of the distinction of being the first woman to make the crossing.

Despite their differences, Harriet did accept one of Hamel's offers. He had warned that she needed a compass, saying, "If you are just five miles off course, you will end up over the North Sea." In that cold and wet emptiness, there was no land, and no way for help to arrive quickly if she ditched into the water. Harriet allowed Hamel to give her a compass, and took a few quick lessons in how to use it.

On Monday, April 15, at 4:00 a. m., there was a knock on Harriet's door. She drank a cup of tea. The sky was dark, chill winds swept the airfield. Harriet and her crew sat in their autos. Then it began to rain. They returned to the hotel.

Tuesday, April 16th. Harriet was called at 3:30 a.m. A half-hour later they were at the airfield. Conditions had improved; the rain had stopped, the wind had calmed. Quickly, attendants brought the monoplane from the hangar. In an hour, they knew, the wind would rise. "Today is the day," Harriet said. Hamel, nodding, jumped in the plane for a short test flight.

A small crowd was gathering. Harriet could see by the look on their faces that they didn't really believe that she, in her "purple suit," was about to fly off over the English Channel. For a moment, she found it difficult to believe it herself. Standing there in the darkness, France seemed very far away. The Channel might have been an ocean. But no, this was the wrong way to think. The Channel had been crossed before, and she would do it now. She was ready.

But was she really? She had never flown the Bleriot before. "All the planes I've flown have had only thirty-horsepower," she found herself saying softly. "This engine has fifty."

Then Hamel landed. "All set?" Leo asked.

"Yes," she answered tersely, "I am."

England was cold in April. The sky over England, and over the Channel, was colder still. In an open cockpit, a pilot's body temperature could drop quickly to a dangerous level. To help combat it, Harriet wore silk "combinations" under her flying suit. On top of her suit she now buttoned a slicker. Woolen gloves, to her elbows, would keep her hands warm. At the last minute, Hamel tied a hot water bottle around her waist, beneath a sheaf of newspapers under her slicker.

"So the *Mirror* is helping me after all," she said.

She climbed into the plane. Smiling, she winked at Ganesha, hanging by a cord from a cockpit strut. Gustav and Leo went through the final preparations. Then the propeller was spun. The cylinders began to fire. White smoke lifted off the valves. It floated past Harriet, and past the six men holding the rudder.

"Good luck!" Hamel shouted. Harriet waved to the crowd. It was 5:39 a.m. The plane hopped a few times across the field and was off. Light was spreading across the sky as Harriet flew the three miles to Dover Castle. She crossed the white cliffs. As she headed out across the Channel, she could see the *Mirror's* tugboat her.

She patted her waist.

# Chapter 9

## Alone In The Fog

Twenty-two miles of water lay between Harriet and Calais. Louis Bleriot had covered it in thirty-six minutes. Harriet looked at her wrist watch. She hoped to do as well as he had done. For a while it seemed as though she would. The plane flew well and the dark Channel seemed to pass below her quickly. Then the fog hit. One moment she could see, and the next moment she could not. Mist and oil smeared her goggles. She took them off, blinking her eyes. Soon she had no sense of where the water was. It could be hundreds of feet away, or inches. Straining to see the altimeter, she climbed the shrieking plane to 5000 feet. Beads of moisture slashed her face like needles. She was sure now that she was above the clouds, but still she could not see. Where was land? Where was France? Had she veered over the North Sea? "The compass," Harriet said, "the compass." She wiped at its glass gripped tightly between her knees.

It read east; she was headed in the right direction. The right direction, Harriet mused. How could anyone flying over the English Channel be flying in the right direction? It is for me, she quickly thought.

Attempting to see beneath her, Harriet dipped the wings. Gasoline flooded the carburetor, stalling the engine. There were long moments of silence as the plane seemed to hang in the sky, long timeless moments when Harriet had no sense of place or direction. Then the pistons caught, roaring back to life and returning Harriet once more to her journey.

According to her watch, she now had been in the air for more than an hour. She had to be over land, or so far from it that she might never see it again. Cautiously, she lowered the plane to 1000 feet. "Ha!" she shouted. The sound seemed to burst from her. "Oh, my!" she exclaimed. There below, to her immense relief, was the most beautiful beach she had ever seen. It was white and long, and quite wonderful. In one hour and nine minutes, Harriet Quimby had flown the English Channel.

After flying inland and failing to find a place to land among the tilled farmland, she headed back to the beach. A group of fishermen looked up to see the plane drop slowly from the sky and settle on the sand. Gesturing among themselves, chattering in French, they carried their pails of worms to a smiling woman dressed in a raincoat and mauve pantaloons. How astounding! In such a place, where every day they threw their lines into the water in the monotonous ritual of fishing.

Placidly, Harriet stepped from the plane. She withdrew the folded copy of the *Mirror* from beneath her slicker. Tearing off a sheet, she wrote a telegram while sitting on the sand. A young boy took the message. "I must pay you later," she told him. He seemed to understand, for he ran off with the paper to the town.

From a nearby life station, a man telephoned Boulogne with the news. Harriet was hungry. She had landed beside the tiny town of Equihen, two miles north of Hardelot, thirty miles from Calais. Because Equihen was such a small village, the press would later designate Hardelot as the landing spot. Harriet, however, would always insist that she had landed near Equihen.

A fisherwoman now brought her a cup of tea and some bread and cheese. She told Harriet to keep the cup as a souvenir. It was large, as big as a tankard, and very old. "I will always treasure this," Harriet told her. The woman then set up a small table and Harriet sat at it, on the white beach, drink-

ing tea and eating the bread and cheese. She looked at the plane. The cooling engine ticked. With a
smile she remembered Ganesha, hanging in the
cockpit. Well, Harriet thought, he had brought her
good luck. She would leave him there a while.

Soon Harriet's friends arrived from Calais.
Laughing, they lifted the pilot onto their shoulders
and carried her across the beach. A photographer
recorded the moment for posterity. Harriet felt
awkward; she felt more comfortable aloft in a plane
than upon the frail shoulders of her friends. The
*Mirror* crew now arrived, bringing Harriet's long
seal stole, which they wrapped about her. They also
brought champagne, toasting Harriet as she posed
in her cockpit.

She was afraid to leave it. Somehow, she had
to get the plane away from the water; the tide was
rising. She spied an elderly man stood among the
small crowd. In halting English, he agreed to help
her. He gathered some of the other men, and they
began pulling the plane to higher ground.

"Come along," said one of Harriet's friends, the
daughter of J. Robinson Whitely. "Tea and cakes
at Mama's." While Harriet went off to "Mama's,"
which turned out to be a mansion, the fishermen
pulled the plane to Bleriot's hangar. Then they and
the local farmers began celebrating. The festivities

continued long after Harriet had left to catch the train to Paris.

Legend has it that the villagers gave Harriet the strip of beach where she had landed and built a small cottage there, in the shape of an airplane. Harriet had not only earned a place for herself in the history books, but also in the hearts of the people of Equihen.

# Chapter 10

## An Unwelcome Return

Harriet now perpared for the headlines. And the headlines certainly came, but not about her. During the cold night of April 14, on its maiden voyage, the *Titanic*, the world's largest ocean liner, struck an iceberg and sank within hours, taking 1,502 lives with it. The *Titanic* was the most luxurious ship ever built, and some of its passengers were among the wealthiest people in Europe and America. Its sinking remained a front-page story for weeks. Harriet's story, a few paragraphs, was on the back pages of most newspapers— except in the *London Daily Mirror*, which had come through with the $5000 promised to Harriet. Her bylined articles in *Leslie's Weekly* did not begin appearing until a month later.

However, despite the public fascination with the *Titanic* tragedy, Harriet did receive a few weeks of moderate praise in Paris and London. Then she and Leo returned to America. On arriving in New York in May with her new seventy-horsepower Bleriot, (which U. S. Customs, not used to airplanes, had designat-ed as a "polo pony"), she expected an enthusiastic welcome. It was not to be. The American public chose to ignore her. What was worse, much of the commentary was negative. Many people were ofended that Harriet was a female. One paper said, "A thing done first is one thing; done for the seventh or eighth time is different. Of course, it still proves ability and capacity, but it does not prove equal-ity." And the *New York Times* added: "The feminists should be somewhat cautious about exalting over Miss Quimby's exploitation, lest by doing so they invite the humiliating qualification, 'great for a woman.'"

The feminists were hardly exalting. Suffrage groups, seeking women's voting rights, came down particularly hard on Harriet. They said there was nothing worse to their movement, besides an anti-suffragette, than an independent woman uninter-ested in their cause. They wanted Harriet to name her plane "The Pankhurst" or "The Catt" after Emmeline Pankhurst and Carrie Chapman Catt, both suffrage leaders. But Harriet, who had earned the money for her plane without the help of the suffragettes, decided to name it the "Genevieve" because she felt the name denoted versatility, a trait she admired. The suffragettes were right: Harriet was an independent woman.

Despite that, it was not easy for her to accept the faint praise of the newspapers. One day she picked up a copy of the *New York Sun*. "The sport is not one for which women are physically qualified," an editorial sniffed. "As a rule, they lack strength and presence of mind and the courage to excel as aviators. It is essentially a man's sport and pasttime."

An angry Harriet waved the paper at Ursula. "How can they say that?" she almost shouted. "I'm not a man. I don't want to be a man. But I'm not lacking in...in..."

"In what?" Ursula said quietly. At seventy-eight, her "bile," as she called it, rose less slowly than it once had.

"Oh, forget it," replied Harriet in frustration.

"No, I won't," insisted Ursula. "And neither will you." she pointed at the newspaper. "Because 'they' won't let us."

Harriet wadded up the paper. "This is enough to make me want to quit."

"Of course it is," Ursula said, walking slowly to her daughter and touching the ball of newspaper. "It's supposed to."

They stood face to face, holding the paper ball. It was as if their eyes met above a light and fragile world. In each other they saw something of themselves.

"Well," Harriet said quietly to her mother. "We have flown a long way from Michigan."

"Yes, and very high," Ursala answered.

Harriet did not give up. With no scheduled promotional tours or financial rewards from her flight, she resumed her job at *Leslie's* at the end of June. Although she greatly enjoyed this type of work, it would not pay for what she had in mind. Her original intention remained: To retire early and write a novel. She would not really be retiring; as a novelist, she intended to work harder than ever. That was what she wanted. A woman of Harriet Quimby's character would not have been content to simply rest.

# Chapter 11

## Courage And Luck

Despite the lack of applause for her Channel flight, Harriet was quickly becoming a recognized authority on aviation; she *was* the aviation editor of one of the largest news magazines in the world. On May 9, 1912, *Leslie's Weekly* released their second issue devoted exclusively to flying. "Birdmen—Evolution of the Airplane," showed a full-page shot of Harriet suited up for her Channel flight.

But contracts for further flights were not materializing. At least one was broken, resulting in a troublesome lawsuit. It was all very frustrating, and Harriet began to think her luck had turned. This frightened her more than had twenty-two miles of open water. After all, luck had played a part in her success, perhaps as much as courage and tenacity. Courage could stay with you, she thought, but when luck departed, you were in—figuratively, if not literally—deep water.

Yet at the same time, she knew this was not true.

There was no such thing as luck. Events were determined by the will of God. All the same, bad luck could not be good for you. It was all very confusing, and Harriet would sit at her desk at *Leslie's* holding the little figure of Ganesha as she tried to decide what to do.

Then she decided. What was right could turn wrong. Good could go bad. Maybe there was no luck, but maybe there was, and there was no point in taking more chances than you had to. Without a word, she got up from her desk, walked from her office to the composing room, and said to a printer, "Cut his head off."

"What?" asked the startled man.

"His head, off with it."

"His li'l elephant head?"

"That's it," Harriet replied, dangling Ganesha from his chain. The idol hung in the air, his arms outstretched, implacable, as if nothing Harriet said or did could affect him. She unhooked the chain.

"Just as you say, Miss Harriet," said the printer, taking the figure from her and carrying it to a work bench. "His head it is, then."

With a flick of his thumb he switched on a band saw; its blade began whirring loudly, reminiscent of a propeller's spin. After eyeing the brass figure professionally, the printer set it on the cutting platform and moved it delicately into the blade. There was a  shearing sound as the blade dug through the metal, almost like a scream, and then the head was gone, flying off the platform toward the floor.

Harriet winced. The printer picked up the head and gave it to her. Then he handed her Ganesha's body.

"Ask me," he said, "it's an improvement."

Harriet looked down at Ganesha.

"Perhaps," she said, "if bad luck can be broken."

Within days, it seemed as if this could be true. Leo had arranged a performance at an air show in Boston from June 29th to July 7th. Harriet was to receive the enormous sum of $100,000 for a seven days at Squantum Airfield. She couldn't believe it; in a few weeks she would have enough money to retire. Leo arranged for another "first." She was to be the first woman to carry the mail by plane, flying non-stop from Boston to New York City on the show's last day. The Postmaster General had sanctioned the flight.

"Your reputation will certainly be made now," a beaming Leo said after breaking the news.

"Oh, Mr. Stevens," replied Harriet, pretending to be unimpressed., "pull your head down from the clouds. Keep your feet on the ground."

Then she took him out for a chicken dinner.

# Chapter 12

## "I Am A Cat"

Just days before the Boston meet, Harriet's former flying instructor paid her a visit at *Leslie's Weekly*. Without taking a seat, Professor Houpert stood in the middle of her office, his bowler hat in his hands, and Harriet knew he wanted to talk about flying. The usually composed man looked so uncomfortable that she half-expected him to examine his anemometer and say, "We must wait."

Instead, he said a thing she would not have predicted. "You must quit," he said. "Please, I beg you."

He told her that Matilde had stopped flying. Almost weekly, it seemed, planes were crashing and pilots dying.

Harriet tried to respond to him brightly. "But André, she said, "You're asking me to hang up my mauve suit."

"This is serious," the professor continued. "No amount of money is worth this... and no amount of fame. I beg that you listen to me."

"I did listen, and you taught me well," she answered. "I am a good pilot, André. It's true, I will be well paid for this show, but that's not why I'm doing it. You know that."

A pained look swept over the professor's face. His fingers strained at his hat brim. "Yes," he said. "I taught you. Of that I am guilty." he turned away. "And I do know why you must fly."

After he had left, Harriet sat quietly for a long while. What she thought of, she could not say.

Harriet looked so stunning in her flying costume that the press started calling her "The Dresden China Aviatrix." With her dark good looks she did not really fit this title, but it stayed with her nonetheless. One critic wrote, "She looks more Spanish than the wholly American girl she declares herself to be," as if there were no Spanish-Americans. Harriet paid little attention to such remarks. The former fashion writer and news photographer had an excellent eye for what looked right on her.

More than eighty years later, Harriet's last few aviation articles have an unintended eerie quality. It was almost as if she were trying to leave an explanation for her apparent flirtation with death. Considering Professor Houpert's admonition, that may well have been the case. She wrote an article for *Good Housekeeping* magazine entitled, "American Bird Woman" in which she said, "Only a cautious person, man or woman, should fly. I do not mount my machine until every wire and screw has been tested. I have never had an accident in the air. It may be luck, but I attribute it to the care of a good mechanic."

Her last article, "Flyers and Flying," on June 27, 1912, provided advice on how to select the proper flight school and find employment in the aviation field. It also contained this important warning: Be on your guard for unexpected dangers.

Harriet was able to make three practice flights in her new Bleriot before shipping it to Boston. She probably was aware that the sleek two-seater had what at least one writer later called an "inherent instability." Several European flyers had met their deaths in this machine.

In her first practice flight, Harriet became the first woman pilot to transport a passenger, Walter Bonner. Later, returning to a Mineloa, N. J., landing field, she raced eighteen-year-old Cecil Paoli, the youngest pilot in the United States, beating him by a plane length. During the third flight, as she was climbing, the Bleriot shot up into the air, dipped a wing and stalled. It began falling uncontrollably, spiraling toward the ground. Although frightened, Harriet neutralized the controls and recovered from the spin. She mentioned the incident to her mechanic, Mr. Hardy, upon landing.

The Harvard-Boston Air Meet promised to be a big event. It was the third such meet held at Squantum Airfield. Many famous flyers were there displaying their bravery and skills: "Daredevil" Lincoln Beachey, "nerveless" Charlie Hamilton, Farnum T. Fish, and the "Queen of the Channel Crossing," Harriet Quimby. The crowd was in awe of these pilots and the excitement was high.

Harriet bantered with her fans and flying colleagues Ruth Law, Blanche Scott, Leo Stevens and another friend, Helen Vanderbilt, were with her. In high spirits, Harriet posed for photographers and gave interviews. She took passengers up for short flights. She made the final preparations for her demonstrations. She also boasted that she intended to beat Claude Grahame-White's above-water speed record of fifty-eight miles per hour, set two years before on Dorchester Bay.

"You don't have to do it," Leo told as they sat in the hangar one afternoon. He had brought her an ice cream cone, which she licked delicately.

"Of course I don't," she said. "But I want to."
Harriet wore a long white dress and a wide round
hat. Leo thought she had never looked more beautiful.

"Ice cream becomes you," he said.

"I'd rather become something else."

"You look nice with it, I mean."

" Leo, how gallant of you," she gently mocked
him. "But I shall still attempt the speed record."

"I'm not being gallant," he insisted.

"I always thought you were."

"I'm being reasonable."

Harriet dabbed at her lips with a napkin. "Not
now, Leo," she said. "Don't be reasonable today."

"You don't need this, Harriet," Leo persisted.
"You've set enough records. Be satisfied with carrying the mail to New York. Then you can retire."

"And write?" she asked.

"That's it."

For long moments Harriet studied the cone. Then
she studied Leo. "Each thing in its place," she said.
"I'll lick this ice cream, then the speed record. Then
I'll taste a novel," she giggled. "And probably take
a licking."

Leo had to laugh with her. Sitting there in the
hangar, he was sure everything would be all right.

\*    \*    \*    \*    \*

Harriet became friendly with the people hosting the show, especially the Willards, Willliam and his son Charles. Charles had been a student at the Wright Brothers' flying school and later one of their demonstration pilots. His father had flown with him many times. William was large, weighing more than 190 pounds.

On the third day of the event, Monday, July 1, Harriet decided to make a trial run over the speed course, from Squantum Field to the Boston Lighthouse and back. It was late in the afternoon, around 5:30, but she still had sufficient light. The twenty-seven mile trip should take less than thirty minutes.

"Which of the Mr. Willards wants a plane ride?" Harriet asked as she stood by her Bleriot, patting a wing. She had on her caped satin flying suit and high-buttoned boots. From her neck, on a silver chain, hung Ganesh.

"I do," they both said quickly. Then everyone grinned. It really had been a wonderful day—perfect flying weather, a large, appreciative audience and, best of all, not a single accident.

"Well," said Harriet, a coy tone to her voice, "don't fight over me. You'll have to decide like gentlemen."

"We'll flip a coin," young Charles said.

"Excellent idea," agreed William.

"Oh, dear," Harriet said, looking away in mock horror. "I detest gambling."

The coin was flipped, and William won.

"I demand a reflip," pouted Charles.

"When we return," said William. He climbed happily into the rear passenger seat.

Before she got in, Harriet spoke briefly to a reporter. He asked how she felt about flying so far over Dorchester Bay.

"A water landing is all right, unless you come down head first," she said. "The heavy motor in the front takes the plane deep in water. But if you can pancake, the broad wings will float it for two or more hours." Then she smiled. "But I am a cat and I don't like cold water." With that, she climbed a short flight of steps and took her seat in the open cockpit.

Four feet behind her, the ample William acted as the plane's ballast; his weight would balance hers on the flight. Without him, the Bleriot would have required sandbags. "Miss Quimby," Willard said, "I'm so glad I won."

"So am I," she teased. "You are somewhat bigger than Charlie."

"Oh, Miss Quimby."

"Oh, Mr. Willard."

"You're marvelous, Miss Quimby."

"Thank you, Mr. Willard. Now hold on."

Harriet untied her cape and tossed it to Leo. She waved to the crowd, which responded with cheers and whistles. Mr. Hardy, at the nose of the airplane, held the propeller. He gave it a pull; it spun, and Harriet switched on the ignition. There was a blast as the engine caught. White smoke blew back. The propeller spun faster. The men at the tail held it tightly. Harriet raised her thumb and the plane roared off, soon lifting high above the crowd. It seemed that all 5000 spectators waved.

The Bleriot rose quickly from 500 to 2000 feet before Harriet leveled it off over the water. Beneath her, Dorchester Bay shone in the sunlight. To the crowd, the Bleriot looked like a white, soaring bird.

Harriet and her passenger flew past a series of small islands. Below, sea gulls rode the air currents. Sailboats cut across the bay. Then Harriet banked the plane around the lighthouse and headed back toward the field. The practice flight was going well. When time came, Harriet was certain, she would break Graham-White's record. Soon the field was beneath her, and she looped it at seventy miles per hour. All the while, Mr. Willard did as she had instructed; he held on. There was little else he could do. There was no seat belt to grasp, no controls to adjust. There was just the immensity of the sky, the howl of the engine and, a few feet away, the narrow back of the pilot, draped in mauve satin. Yes, he thought, she is marvelous.

The crowd froze as the plane seemed to wobble for a moment in the breeze. Then it straightened out and flew past the airfield and around the Savin Hill Yacht Club. Now, after flying for twenty minutes, Harriet slowly began her descent. Carefully, she wiped the oil from her goggles.

This was the finest aeroplane ride William had ever taken. Splendid, he kept thinking to himself. He really must tell her. "You are doing wonderfully, Miss Quimby," he shouted. She did not respond she must not have heard. "Splendid!" he shouted again. Still, no response. The plane was dropping quickly, angling toward the earth. Well, he thought, if I must, I'll simply tap her shoulder. He began to do just that, straightening up from his seat and leaning forward to touch her.

As he did so, the nose of the plane lurched suddenly downward, the tail flew up, and William was thrown into the bright and soft air just as he said again the word "splendid." And it was, somehow, splendid, leaving the noise of the plane, the vibrating seat, the airplane's clumsiness. For a second, before he started his fall, large William felt as weightless as a cloud.

Harriet too was thrown forward, slamming her chest and arms against the frame of the cockpit. Her breath left her lungs and she felt herself hanging forward, staring straight down at the ground. Blinking her eyes, she tried to reach for the controls. But her arms would not move; they were broken. Helpless, she could do nothing but wait as the airplane slid upside down, and felt herself sliding out of the seat. She fell away from the plane, over and over, tumbling through the air toward the water. She hit it before Willard.

Among the crowd, Leo stood watching. He collapsed to his knees. "No," he murmured. He did not see the plane land on its back near the shore, or the boats from the yacht club rush to the bodies. He did, though, see the men bring Harriet and Willard ashore. He looked down as they lay on the beach. Harriet, her eyes open, seemed to look past him at the sky.

# Chapter 13

## Rest, Gentle Spirit

Harriet Quimby and William Willard had fallen into five feet of water in Dorchester Bay, about 200 feet from shore. The plane lay on its back nearby. It was hardly damaged, a few struts and wires broken.

Pilot Blanche Scott had witnessed the accident from the air. She tried to land immediately, but the crowd had rushed onto the field. After two attempts she finally brought her plane down, and needed help to get out.

William's son Charles had to be restrained.

The mud-covered bodies were taken to Quincy Hospital where it was determined that Harriet had died instantly. William may not have. Pressure remained in his lungs. His skull, however, was fractured, as were his and Harriet's spine and legs. There was no way the two could have survived the one thousand-foot fall.

Harriet's death shocked the nation. Unlike her
Channel crossing, she now made headlines. No one
was sure of the cause of the crash. Some said it
was the mechanic's fault. He disagreed.

"The machine lost its balance," Mr. Hardy said.
"I personally tested every screw, bolt and wire before we pushed the machine from the hangar."

Theories abounded.some said an air pocket had
caught the plane and allowed it to drop. Lincoln
Beachey thought Harriet had fainted or lost her grip.
Leo Stevens thought the accident occurred when
William Willard leaned forward. He knew her flying abilities well, and most people accepted his
explanation. It is as fitting as any.


The air meet continued for the rest of the week.
Some of the planes flew black crepe banners and
the pilots wore black armbands. From having started with so much promise, the meet ended  $30,000
in debt. Authorities revealed that the show had been
unsanctioned, and the licenses of seven flyers were
subsequently suspended.

Harriet's parents arrived in Boston by train on
the evening of her death. It was difficult for them
to accept what had happened, that their talented and

beautiful daughter had come to this. Harriet's body was moved to a Quincy funeral home where, the next morning, the Quimbys, with Leo Stevens and Helen Vanderbilt, viewed the remains. Looking at her daughter, Ursula remembered the child on the farm in Michigan. She recalled the vibrant young woman announcing that she would be a writer. And she recalled Harriet's words: "I want to fly."

Harriet's flying career was brief. She had died a month short of the anniversary of her pilot's license. The *Boston Post* said of her: "Harriet was ambitious to be among the pathfinders. She took her chances like a man and died like one." In the last article she ever wrote, "Lost In The Sky," found in her desk at *Leslie's*, Harriet had inserted, at the end, a message to her parents. It said that if ill fortune should befall her, she would meet her fate rejoicing. *Leslie's* printed the article on November 28, 1912. Its final words comforted her friends as well as her family. Often she had told those who knew her that she did not fear death, for she believed it led to a fadeless immortality.

No copy of an autopsy was found. The cause of death remains unconfirmed. While she lay in the morgue, her satin flying suit and antique jewelry were stolen. Ursula was enraged by this. She had intended to donate them to the Smithsonian Institution. Later she would claim that more of Harriet's jewelry, six gold rings and an Egyptian necklace, were stolen from a trunk in her hotel room.

Harriet was buried in Woodlawn Cemetery in New York on July 5, 1912. Because she had feared that her body would be taken by doctors for experiments, she was laid to rest in a burglar-proof vault, lined with copper.

On August 8, 1912, *Leslie's Weekly* solicited donations to purchase a stone monument for her grave. Hundreds of dollars poured in. Her remains were exhumed on Octber 23, 1913. Leo, with the approval of the Quimbys, had Harriet reburied at the Kensico Cemetery in Valhalla, New York. A monument was placed on her grave a few months later. Its inscription reads: "Harriet Quimby—The first woman in America to receive a pilot's license to fly. The first woman in the world to fly a monoplane alone across the English Channel, April 16, 1912. The life of the heroic girl went out when she fell with her passenger aeroplane at Boston, July 1, 1912. She was the Dramatic Editor of Leslie's Weekly. REST GENTLE SPIRIT."

Omitted from the inscription was the date of her birth.

Harriet's relationship with Leo was never made clear. It is known that he married twice during his lifetime, and presumed that he was single during the few months he knew Harriet. Evidently, he and Harriet had a close commitment to each other. He cared about her, and was more than her mere business partner. Some say that Harriet loved John Moisant. If so, she loved him briefly, because he died soon after they met. Harriet herself died unmarried and childless. At thirty-seven, she was well-known in the United States and Europe. Had she lived, she would certainly have set more aviation records and firsts. She might have attempted the first flight across the Atlantic Ocean

But when Harriet died, she fell into an  unjust obscurity.  For decades she was virtually forgotten. Her accomplishments, however, were remarkable, and it has only been during the past few years that this has been acknowledged. The Smithsonian Institution now displays her picture, and in 1994, the U. S. Postal Service issued a commemorative stamp A few encyclopedias now include her. Coldwater, Michigan, honors her with a marker and preserves data on her in its library.

Ursula died in May, 1916, and was buried next to Harriet. William died in February, 1922, at the age of eighty-seven. He was buried in Greenville, Michigan. The fate of Harriet's sister Kitty is unknown.

Matilde Moisant never spoke of Harriet, which adds to the mystery of Harriet's life. Matilde was eighty-five when she died in 1964. Her birthdate, like Harriet's, has been questioned.

Harriet can rightly be criticized for such things as lying about her age. She was superstitious, and defaced a religious object—the figure of Ganesha— revered by millions of Hindus. She openly sought notoriety and wealth. She was ambitious; she took dangerous risks. Yet, today, when young women expect much more out of life than they did in earlier days, Harriet's story can serve as both a source of pride and hope. We all can be proud there were courageous women like her, and we can only hope that there will be many more.

Harriet looked hard at her society, and wrote accurately of her observations, but she obviously was thinking of the future when she predicted:

"The day is coming when vast thousands of people will span the oceans in comfort and safety in giant aeroplanes to the distant capitols of our world neighbors."

Skeptics at the time replied, "You're out of your mind. Airships will never be more than toys for the rich...and bring death to young fools."

They were wrong. She was right.

# Bibliography

## Books

Adams, Jean and Kimball. *Heroines of the Sky*. N, Y., Doubleday, 1942.

Hall, Ed. *Harriet Quimby: America's First Lady of the Air*. Spartanburg, S. C., Honoribus Press, 1993.

Holden, Henry. *Her Mentor Was An Albatross*. Mt. Freedom, N.J., Black Hawk Publishing Co., 1993.

Mondey, D. *Women of the Air*. London: Wyland Publishers, 1981.

Oaks, Claudia M. *United States Women in Aviation Through WWI*. Washington, D.C.: Smithsonian Studies in Air and Space, vol. 2, 1979.

## Periodicals

"Fatal Aeroplane Accident at Boston." *Scientific American*, July 12, 1912.

Gregory, Elizabeth Hiatt. "Women's Records in Aviation." *Good Housekeeping*, September, 1912.

"Harriet Quimby, America's First Woman Aviator." *Overland Monthly Magazine*, December, 1911.

Jones, Terry Gwynn. "For A Brief Moment The World Seemed Wild About Her." *Smithsonian Magazine*, January, 1984.

Ovington, Earl. "Explanation of Quimby Accident." *Scientific American*, July 20, 1912.

Quimby, Harriet. "American Bird Woman. *Good House-

*keeping*. June, 1912.

_____. "How A Woman Learns to Fly." *Leslie's Illustrated Weekly*, March 25, 1911; Part III, August 17, 1911.

_____. "How I Won My Aviator's License." *Leslie's Illustrated Weekly*, August 24, 1911.

Semple, Elizabeth Ann. "Harriet Quimby: America's First Woman Aviator." *Overland Monthly Magazine*, December, 1911.

"To Reduce Aviation Fatalities." *Literary Digest*, July 13, 1912.

Wilcox, Shirley. "Aviatrix Harriet Quimby: She Showed The Way." *American History Illustrated*, November, 1985.


## Newspapers

"Dead Woman's Jewels Gone." *New York Times*, February 7, 1915.

"Miss Harriet Quimby." *East Delineator*, November, 1911.

"Miss Harriet Quimby Born This County." *Daily Courier* (Coldwater, Michigan), July 3, 1912.

"Miss Quimby Dies in Airship Fall." *New York Times*, July 2, 1912.

"Miss Quimby Flies English Channel." *New York Times*, April 16, 1912.

"Miss Quimby Wins Air Pilot License." *New York Times*, August 1, 1911.

"Settle Quimby Estate." *New York Times*, August 13, 1915.

## Other Sources

Hughes, Alice. Former librarian of Branch District Library, Coldwater, Michigan.

Koontz, Giacinta Bradley, ed. *The Harriet Quimby Research Conference Journal, Vol. 1*. Woodland Hills, CA, 1995.

Lynch, Maureen. Vintage airplane researcher. Glen Falls, New York.

# Index